MY EYES ON YOU

Porsha Preyer

Daniel Sumo

[signature]

Thank you for your support.
With God all things are possible.

Published by Passion Publications - a division of
Tell the Truth International
7005 Woodbine Ave
Sacramento, Ca. 95822
tellthetruthsac@gmail.com

Printed in the United States of America
© 2021 by Daniel Sumo

Cover image and design by:
charlyn_designs@fiverr.com

ISBN: 978-0-9729904-9-3

CONTENTS

ACKNOWLEDGMENTS

To my Mother Felekpai Sumo: She's one of the greatest main characters of this book. As Prince Nico said in his song, "When I was hungry, my mother could run, that she could find me something to chop (eat)." When I was desperately wanting to go to school, my mother left to sleep in the bush for one year because she sold all her clothes to pay my school fee. She encouraged me to get rid of fear. She advised me to always do the right thing. My mother did not receive an academic education, but she is an extraordinary caring mother when it comes to meeting her children's needs in life. She would never eat if I had not eaten or if I were still outdoors. Mother, I thank God for you.

Professor Moses Y. Yarkpawolo: When I was rejected by a family member, after he had promised to help me continue my education in the city, Yarkpawolo, who is my uncle, accepted me to live with him in Monrovia. He allowed me to work with him in his office as a volunteer and he taught me how to use the mimeograph machine.

Celestine G. Teekeh: This lady took me in like her own biological son when I was going to school to obtain my high school diploma. In the school, if I had not eaten, Mrs. Teekeh would not eat. She gave me money for food at the end of every week for Saturday and Sunday. She gave me great encouragement to be faithful while I was pursuing my high school education.

Dorothea M. Quiena: Dorothea took care of me as her own son. Dorothea embraced me with love, care, and honor. She took the place of Mrs. Teekeh and cared for me with Godly love. She gave me the right advice and monitored my daily activities to make sure I was doing the right thing. Dorothea prayed with me every day whenever she entered the school. When I got the opportunity to travel to the United States, I did not have money to buy the plane ticket. Dorothea took her last money she had in her account and gave it to me to buy my plane ticket to travel before my visa to America would expire.

Charlotte J. Sumo: Charlotte J. Sumo is my wife God blessed me with from the United States. She was the strong leading force in helping me to write this book and getting me to where I am today. She sustained me in ways I never knew I needed. My wife diligently stood by me, encouraging me day and night to write this book. She helped me with my vocabulary when I encountered difficulty putting my ideas together for this book. This book could not have been completed without her encouragement and support. Charlotte Sumo, I thank the Almighty God for having you in my life.

Pastor Benjamin Marshall: Writing a book is harder than I thought and more rewarding than I could have ever imagined. None of this would have been possible without my pastor, Benjamin Marshall. Pastor Marshall is not only a pastor but also a missionary who travels to many countries. I am eternally grateful to my pastor who was willing to adjust his busy schedule of studying, praying, counseling, and planning so this book could be published.

FOREWORD

I HAD THE PLEASURE OF meeting Daniel in the fall of 2015. Since that time, we have grown in our admiration for each other. I have found him to be a God-fearing man who not only loves God but people. We have been privileged to travel together on missionary trips back to his native country of Liberia. He and his family recently moved near our ministry headquarters to be a part of our mission ministry work.

As I worked with Daniel on getting his biography ready for public distribution, I was inspired to say the least. There is no possible way I can prepare you for such an amazing story. This book will astound you as it testifies to how great God truly is and how His hand will not stop at any length from protecting, providing, delivering, and blessing those who love Him and place their trust in Him. Time after time God helps Daniel in his afflictions.

Daniel shows us how beneficial it is to fear God and live righteously. This is the kind of role model our youth in Liberia need along with the rest of our world. People with character that is seen by their respect, honesty, truthfulness, generosity, kindness, and humility are hard to find these days. It is a breath of fresh air when you find such a person. Liberia will be a transformed place when we can get the youth to imitate this type of behavior.

Lastly, what I love most about Daniel is the passion we share about the country of Liberia, its people, and those like them around the globe. We both desire to do all we can to see lives transformed for the glory of God. Thanks Daniel, for the hope so many will receive from your story and for reminding the world that God is alive, watching us all the time, and truly able to save us out of all our troubles.

Benjamin Marshall
President of Tell the Truth International
Pastor, Author, Missionary

INTRODUCTION

THERE ARE SO MANY situations in the world that can hold people down in one place to stop them from moving forward. Some of these situations are:

- Family disappointments
- Academic or career disappointment
- Financial crises
- Being denied your rights
- Criticism from people
- Facing a disaster
- Lack of support
- Disappointment in friendship
- Rejection
- Feeling like your life has no meaning
- Getting older with no career
  ....and many more.

If you are in such a situation or if you have ever found yourself in such a situation, know that there is a better day yet to come; no condition is permanent.

This book focuses on how I successfully made it from growing as a young boy to where I am today. As a young person growing up, there are many expectations of being successful that come to one's mind. Many of these include success in business, finances, and feeling worthy and important.

What is success? Success is defined in the western dictionary as favorable or prosperous. This may include a person of great financial worth. From the Christian perspective, success simply means that you have Christ in your life; Jesus is first in your life every day. If Christ is your daily focus in life, you will be successful in every good thing you desire. As Matthew 6:33 says, "But seek first the kingdom of God and his righteousness and all these things will be added to you."

CHAPTER 1

Early Life

I WAS BORN IN THE year 1977 to the union of Mr. and Mrs. Sumo in a little village call Beletandla. I am from a family of seven in number. My brother Elijah and I were born as twins, but he became the older brother of me and the third born of the seven children. Even though my mother was pregnant with me and my brother Elijah at the same time, Elijah has a different birth date from mine. When my mother was pregnant with me and my brother, she did not know that she had two babies in her stomach.

My parents lived in a village where there was no medical facility. Due to the lack of a medical facility in the village, my mother did not check herself into a hospital during the time of her pregnancy. Not only did she not know that she was pregnant with twins, but no one else knew either. When my mother was in labor pains, traditional women called midwives who have been specifically trained to assist in childbirth, came and spent time with mother until she gave a natural birth with my brother Elijah. They never knew she had another baby that was left in her stomach, which was me. After two weeks, my mother began to experience severe pain in her stomach. The midwives boiled a leaf, considered as a country pain medication, and brought the water to her as medicine to drink but it did not help the pain in her stomach.

They took her to the Phebe hospital, which was two hours away from the village. When they got her at the hospital, she was admitted that very night. After the doctor examined her, he realized that she was still pregnant with another baby in her stomach. They kept my mother in the hospital for another two days without any sign of delivering me, then the doctor prescribed a C-section delivery for her to deliver.

MY TRADITIONAL NAME

When my mother delivered me, they did not have any name selected for me, because I was a surprise. The first thought of my parents was to name me after one of my grandparents. The first name that was given to me was Mokobaa, which was my grandfather's nickname from my father's side of the family. We stayed at the hospital for one week. After we left the hospital and came back to our village, a traditional Zoe man, who was one of the traditional leaders of the village, asked my parents to name me after him with the name Kolibah. My parents agreed to give me the name because they believed that it was an honor to name your child after the village leader. I was called by the name Kolibah until I turned the age of fifteen.

When I was ten years old, I began to wonder about the meaning of this name Kolibah. I asked my parents to show me the meaning and why they gave me this name. They did not give me any information concerning this name, but only I was named after one of the village leaders who was Zoe (leader of the men secret society known as Pora).

Since I did not get any clear information from my parents about this name, I decided to ask other people in the village to show me the meaning of the name. They did not tell me the meaning of the name either, but only told me the reason why that name should be given to a person. This was their answer: "If a man is named Kolibah, that means he is the leader of the voodoo and the person responsible to make every decision of the traditional Poro Society." Upon hearing this, I told my parents that I did not want to be called that name anymore. My mother tried to convince me to keep it by saying this name was given to you by a known leader in the land and he who bears that name cannot face any problems in the community. I did not accept it. I continued to bother my parents to change my name for many months, but they would not change it.

GOD CHOSE ME

My father and mother were not fortunate enough to achieve education; therefore, they invested their lives in subsistence farming to take care of us. They could not get enough money to sponsor us in school. My uncle, who was the only educated man from my mother siblings, decided to help some of his sister's children as well as other family members.

After the selection of boys and girls was made by my uncle, I was not one of the ones selected to be sponsored by him. Those of us who were not selected by my uncle, were to be left in the village as wine makers to provide palm wine for those brothers, sisters, and cousins who were now living in the city with my uncle. Whenever they would come down into the interior during vacation, they were given the responsibility to bring us clothes, shoes, and other things.

Every day I would always cry to my parents that I wanted to go to school. Anytime I started crying, my mother would always offer the best food to me and say, "Son not everybody can be educated. Since you are the only one staying here, you will always get things from the family that come from the city for vacation."

In the village, it was hard for every parent to get money to pay their children's school fees. However, the school in the village was a public school and the student's tuition and fees payment could be paid with other things besides money.

Students who did not have money to pay for their education would usually take their garden tools to the school such as hoes, axes, machetes, and shovels to show them to the principal. If the students could show they had farming tools, they allowed them to attend the village school. My parents always made sure tools were available for me so I can go to school since they did not have any money to send me there. This is how I lived in the interior with my parents while going to the village school to learn how to write my name.

While I was with my parents, I was still interested in going to the city to receive an education. Every two or three weeks I would be constantly asking my parents if I will ever go into the city to continue my education. One day my mother sent a message to her sister and told her that I was continually crying because I was not chosen to go with my uncle into the city for school. My aunt decided to take me to live with her and her husband. My aunt registered me in a public school where she was living. She lived in a more developed area, so the school was better than my village school. She told one of her older stepsons, who was also in the same school as I, to take care of me always while I am in school.

SAVED IN THE RIVER

Her older stepson, Phillip, was not so responsible. Each day when school was over, he and the other big schoolboys would always go to the creek to swim. He would always leave me with one older lady who was in the town. Afterward, he would take me back on the farm to my aunt.

On a particular day, after we got out of school, there was nobody available to watch me in the town while they were going to swim. The lady I usually stayed with had gone to visit her family members in another village. Phillip said to me, "There is nobody for me to leave you with today, therefore you are going with me to the creek and you are going to learn how to swim."

So, when I went with them to the creek, all of them jumped in the water to swim and I was sitting beside the water watching them swim. Phillip, the boy who my auntie left in charge of me, told me to jump in the water so he can teach me how to swim. I said, "No! the water is deep, it will overtake me if I jump in it." Phillip said, "The water is not deep and swam a little farther in the water, wobbling and floating over it like he was standing on a solid ground. When I saw him wobbling over the water, I believed that the water was not so deep, and he was standing over a solid object.

I decided to jump there to him, but I could not feel anything solid to stand on and I started sinking under the water. He tried to rescue me, but he could not hold me up and swim at the same time. So, he tried to let me go but I was holding him so tight that he could not move. He fought hard to get me off him and I was left alone with nothing to hold on to. I could not stand or swim. The water current began to carry me far down the creek. I tried to swim. I began throwing my hands over me to grab on to something, but I could not find anything. After the water had carried me far down the creek, I was very much helpless. I just happened to put my hand over me reaching out for something and grabbed some rope hanging from a tree branch over the water. It was strong and I was able to remain holding on until some people came to rescue me.

When they took me to my auntie and explained the whole situation to her, she got so upset with me and her stepson. She kept me there with her for a few days until I could fully recover to my old self. After that, she took me back to my mother by the end of that week.

MY EYES ON YOU

When I was in school in the Village, I used to walk thirty miles from the farm to the town for school every morning. In many African countries, many people make their subsistence farming far away from the town, while others make their farm close to the town. People who make farms far away from the town decide to sleep on their farms so they can keep wild animals from destroying the crops.

My parents were some of those who always made their farm far from the town. During farming season, they always slept on the farm. The farming season was at the same time our school opened in the village. I was one of the students in the village school and my parents and I were sleeping on the farm to take care of the rice we planted from being destroyed by the birds. When our parents plant the rice, it is the responsibility of their teenage children to stop the birds from destroying the rice.

In 1993, my parents had planted a large farm with rice. During this season, my school had just opened in the village. Our school hours always started at 8am and ended at 2pm. Since I was in school in the morning hours, my parents told me that I will be responsible to stop the birds from eating the rice in the evening between 5pm to 8:30pm. My parents decided it would be best for me to sleep on the farm with them afterward, then travel to go to school in the morning, since my time to stop the birds was much later.

My parents planned for me to get up in the morning at 5am to go into the village for school. I was always getting up at 5am to walk in the dark to go into the village for school. The distance from the farm to the village was two hours walking distance. When I started going the very first week, it was so hard for me because I was always afraid to walk alone in the dark. My mother tried to encourage me by telling me that I will see some other children on the road going to school since that was the farming season time. I walked on the road for the first two weeks without seeing anyone.

So, I decided I would drop myself from going to school, but my daddy and mom decided to encourage me in a different way. Each time I decided to leave at 5am to go to town for school, my father or my mother would always say one thing to me that would make me no longer afraid to travel in the darkness. One of them would always tell me, "*Go son, my eyes is on you.*" When I heard this word from one of my parents, I would then be able to walk for 2 hours distance with no fear because I knew my mother's or father's eyes were on me. I walked on that forest road so many times with no fear because of my parent's words to me.

One morning while going to school between 5:45am to 6am, I arrived at a certain place on the road and saw something big lying across the road like a log. I did not know what it was. I had passed this spot many times before and it had never been there. I wanted to go back home, but my father had brought me across the river creek with the canoe to start my walk to school, and he had already returned to the farm on the other side of the river. Every morning he would do this and afterschool after my long walk, when I reached the river, I would catch a ride on a canoe with someone and return home.

So, I started thinking that if I go back now, nobody will be there to take me across the river since it was so early in the morning. I decided to walk in the bushes to get to the other side of this long looking log, but I guess I did not know how long it really was. I decided to jump over it instead of walking in the bush in the dark. I took many steps back to get a running start. I then begin to run toward it and once I got close to it, I jumped with hard speed and landed on the other side and kept running as hard as I could until I reached the town.

I went to school that day. After school was over, I went back to the farm on that same road, passing the same spot but did not see what I saw there that morning. When I arrived at my parent's farm, I told my mother about what I had seen. She would never ever allow me to sleep on the farm during a school day again. She would have my father walk me all the way into the village after I finished my chore keeping the birds from the rice. I did not know what it was on the road that day, but everyone who I told the story believed it was a boa constrictor (snake), including my mom. I was more than lucky, not only did I believe my parent's eyes were on me, when I look back, I now know God's eyes were on me too.

THE PALM TREE

During the rainy season, palm oil is always scarce in Liberia because it is not the season for palm bearing fruit. The palm trees are usually wet and slippery, making it hard for harvesters to climb up the trees to get the fruit. Many of the young people who do this work are not brave enough to go into the bush to harvest the palm fruit for oil. At the time, many neighborhoods could not afford to buy oil because it was now expensive at the market. Due to the scarcity of palm oil, my uncle's wife decided to contact young people from our village area who would produce oil for her on the farm and she would buy a bicycle for them in return.

At that time, I knew how to climb up the palm tree to cut palm fruit and since I needed and wanted a bicycle, I decided to sign up and take her up on her offer. I wanted this bicycle so desperately that I could not wait to produce the quantity of oil requested by her. The day was on a Sunday where we were all deciding to go to church. I decided that since this is on a Sunday and many of the young boys who knew how to climb palm trees and cut palm fruit were going to church right then, I would get a head start and have less competition by going into the bush to find and cut palm fruit now.

That Sunday morning, I decided to go into the bush to look for palm fruit to harvest for my bicycle. I decided to leave unknown to my parents because I knew if my mother knew she would try to force me to go with them to church instead of allowing me to go into the bush to look for palm fruit. However, my mother heard that I had decided to go into the bush to harvest palm. She called me in the house and told me that today is not a good day for me to go into the bush to harvest palm. She said to me, "Why don't you wait until tomorrow and go to church today?" I accepted her advice but planned to go later unknown to her.

I waited until my mother went in the shower then I quickly grabbed my palm tree climber and my spear and left secretly with my little brother to go in the bush to harvest palm. My little brother asked me, "Did you tell our mother?" I said to him, "No, because I don't want her to know anything about this to stop me." I told him to quickly follow me; running to leave the town before my mother could see me. I did not realize I was running from sound advice, good direction, and from a safe place while running to danger, the wrong direction, and much trouble. I was headed out like a bird about to go into a net without realizing it or like a deer running to be caught in a trap. I did not know that there was danger ahead of me. I did not realize that what I was doing was a big mistake. I needed to listen to my mother. I should have known it was more important to seek God and His kingdom and righteousness, then all these things I wanted would be added unto me. I had only one thing on my mind; to get the bicycle.

I went to the neighbor's farm. This farm had just been recently burned. I saw a palm tree that was full and bear with its fruit, ripe with eight heads of palm fruit on it, and ready to be harvested. Under this palm tree there were a lot of big pieces of wood stumps from trees that had just been cut down to make room for farming.

This palm tree was about 40 feet tall. When I climbed up this palm tree, it was difficult for me to turn left and right because some of the palm branches got caught in the climber. I took off the spear from my arm and tried to take out the palm branch from the climber. I barely had time to push the spear under before the palm branches broke away from the climber. One of those branches caused the climber to go up, and the climber came out from under me. I felt myself coming down from the palm tree with my head down.

My little brother, who I took with me, saw me coming down but did not know what to do. I got to the ground so hard and broke my back, my two hands and my head got stuck between two wooden tree stumps. My little brother was so afraid, he did not come close to me but ran to the nearby farm yelling for help. When the people came, I was very much unconscious. I did not even know where I was or what was going on around me. The people took me and put me in a hammock and carried me into the town. There was no hospital facility in the village. There was no transportation. The closest motor car on the road for me to ride in was about a ten-hour walking distance from the village where I was.

However, there was a country doctor in the neighbor village who knew how to treat broken bones. This man was known in the village as a professional country bone doctor who had a history of treating many people who had any broken bone problems in the community. My parents sent for him to come and treat my broken back and hands, but he refused to come because he was holding a grudge against my father. He said my father had done something to him when they were younger, for that reason he will not do anything for me, my father, nor any of his family.

My father's uncle, who was a chief, ended up sending word to him to forget about every grudge that he is holding against my father and come to help me. When he received the message, he sent a word back to him that he will be there the next day. When that day came, he did not come. The following day he came, and I was really suffering. I had been in the same painful, broken condition for three days without any treatment. I was crying all night and could not sleep because I was in so much pain. My body was very swollen.

The doctor boiled leaves in a pot and begin to warm my broken hands and back. He did this for two days. He told my father that he was returning home, but he was leaving my father in charge of the medication. My father was to continue warming my two broken hands and back. My father continued to warm my broken hands and back, but there was no improvement. My hands and back continued to swell and the pain got worse every day because my father did not know what to do. My parents sent the doctor a message that my hands were not improving. When the doctor returned, he got mad with my father blaming him for letting my hands get more damaged and saying there is nothing he can do about it. Then he told my parents that the only solution he can do is to re-break my hands and fix it.

He scheduled the re-breaking of my hands which was the next day. When that day came, he got ready to re-break my hands to fix them, and I will never forget it because it was the most painful experience in my life. When he grabbed my swollen hands, he twisted left and right to break it. It was so painful that the pain I felt that day can never be described. He spent two weeks there working on my re-broken hands and back, but I could never get my hands back to its original God created form. Since my hands could not be healed to the original form, he told me that I will just have to be exercising my hands all the time in life. I would also not be able to do any farm work with my hands anymore. The only opportunity I believed I had, from that day forward, was to get into a school where I could get a good education. How would I learn and help myself in life when my parents did not have the money to send me to school so I can get my diploma? This was one of the most frustrating situations I had ever faced in my life while growing up as a child. This situation only caused me to want to be educated even more.

CHAPTER 2

The Effect of the Liberian Civil War

IN 1990 A CIVIL war entered Liberia, this war started between two Liberian tribes and took over the country. When this war started, I was 13 years old and still living with my parents in the village. We heard about the war but did not believe it because it was the first time any of us experienced war between two different ethnic groups in the same country. The rebel group called the National Patriotic Front of Liberia (NPFL) was led by Charles Taylor. Before this war extended into the center of Liberia, the rebel leader and some of his group had a misunderstanding that caused the group to be divided. One group went one way led by the mean rebel leader Charles Taylor. The other group, who went another way, was led by Prince Y. Johnson and was called the International Patriotic Front of Liberia (INPFL).

Prince Johnson took his group and traveled to the western part of the country, which is located near the village where I was born. In 1991, these rebels entered my village for the first time. At that time, my parents and I were on the farm where we usually made our rice garden. When it was noontime, a few of these rebels entered the farm while we were there. They asked us to leave from the farm immediately and go into the town. We did exactly as they told us. When we entered the town, the town was so crowded with rebels that were led by Prince Y. Johnson along with the town citizens. They put everybody in one line to list everyone's name in the town and to know who the young boys and girls were among the group.

This was their way of collecting the young people in every village or town they entered to be a part of their rebel group and to train them while they were traveling. Whenever they came into a town or village, they spent one or two weeks there training boys and girls to be a part of them. One morning, after they had spent three days in our town, they collected boys and girls for training. Many of us young boys and girls escaped and hid in various locations in the town, but they searched until they found us. When they arrested us to go under rebel training, a few boys and I decided to go and appeal to the leader to relieve us from the training.

When we approached the leader, he yelled out with these words: "NO, MY MISSION IS IMPORTANT THAN ANYTHING UNDER THIS EARTH, NO MAN OR WOMAN CAN EVER BE EXCUSED FROM IT EXCEPT DEATH." Then he passed an order that we should be kept in jail until his departure. We were all arrested and placed in jail for three days.

When they were about to leave, those of us who requested to be released were commanded to carry the ammunition boxes first. After they took us from the jail, we walked in a single line straight to the ammunition warehouse. When

35

we got there, I was the first person they assigned with another man from another village to take one of the biggest ammunition boxes. The man and I agreed that one person will take the box from one location to another and let the other take it from that location to another. We agreed with that plan, so I was the first to take the box and travel with it about 25 miles per hour, and we got to a creek with a bridge over it for people to cross.

The water creek was so full that nobody could easily cross it by walking in it. The rebel leader Prince Johnson said nobody is walking in the bridge with his supplies, everybody should walk in the water to cross. The water was about 5 feet 2 inch deep, and I am only 5 feet 1 inch tall. I started to think how will I walk in a water that is 5 feet 2 inch deep if I am only 5 feet 1 inch tall? I started walking in the water with the ammunition box on my head, when I was approaching the deeper part of the water, it was already up to my neck, so I decided to lift the ammunition box with my two hands and lift my noise in the air at the same time. I walked in the water with my whole body under the water while lifting the box with my hand until I crossed the water. I called my partner to come and take it from there to the next location.

I stood there on the side to take the wet clothes off me. When I lifted my head, I realized my partner had took the box and left me. When I realized he was already gone, I started to chase him, but he was already gone too far. While running to reach him, I stopped to look behind and I saw nobody coming. I also looked ahead of me and saw nobody, so I decided to run in the bush to escape. I went far into the bush until I reached back by the water again. I decided I would hide in the bush and stay there until all of them had passed by and then I would race myself back home. While I was sitting there, I saw three of the rebels coming toward me, there was no way for me to escape because the water was full all around the bush and I could not run toward them either.

I slowly got into the water and went under the water where a little bush was covering the water. They came and sat where I was sitting. I was under the water with my face up in the air to receive oxygen. I stayed still until they smoked their cigarette and left. After they left, I spent another 45 minutes in the water before coming out. I came out and sat for another one hour.

I listened so carefully and did not hear anybody passing or talking so I left and took another road to go back home. When I got home at 10:30pm, my mother who had cried all day for me, began to rejoice. She hugged me so tight with great joy and held me up in her arms for five minutes. She said this word to me "My son, God gave you to me as a gift, I knew my gift was coming back to me." She then started to bless me with these words: "God gave you to me as a gift, God gift is perfect, it never fails, and it never be defected. Since God gave you to me, I will now protect you like a hen protecting her children with her wing."

FRESH HUMAN HEART SOUP

After Prince Johnson's rebels had passed through our village, we did not experience any rebel activity for about one year and a half. We could hear fighting going on far away, but it was not near our area. The war went on from 1990 until 1992 with no sign of rebels coming into our village. We thought the civil war was already over and it would never reach our village again.

Suddenly, one evening we saw the first NPFL rebels, who were under the command of Charles Taylor. They came and took control of the whole clan and its surroundings areas. They employed soldiers in every village in the clan and decided to be there permanently. They made my village as one of their headquarters. We were all living with these rebels in my village peacefully.

In April 1992 at 5am while we were all in bed, we heard a lot of gunshots from a far distance, the leaders of the villagers came together to inform everybody to leave the town to go to their various farms. My parents and I left and went on our farm where we considered hiding ourselves. We were there for three days when we saw a group of rebels come and tell us to leave from the farm and go into the town. We left and went to the town. When we entered the town, the whole town was full again with another rebel group called Unimo.

These rebel soldiers who captured the town from the NPFL soldiers, ordered every young boy and girl to join them to fight, but at that time I was now the evangelist over the Lutheran church because the pastor of the Lutheran church had left the town with his family and took refuge in another country. Since I was now heading the church, they excused me from being a part of the rebel soldiers and let me and my family go home.

Then the next day the rebels passed an order that nobody can go on the farm or in any bush for one month. While we were in the town for the two weeks everybody was out of food. Only the rebel soldiers could get food because they were the only ones going to the various farms.

One morning at the hour of 10am, the other rebel group that was sent on the battle front came from the battle front with a fresh human being's heart. They brought this human heart to cook it and eat as a soup. They entered my parents' house with this human heart and asked me to provide pepper for their human heart soup, but we did not have any pepper in the house because we had not gone on the farm for two weeks. "I would be willing to give you pepper for your soup, but we have not gone on the farm for two weeks," I said. "Every cooking materials we have here is finished, there is no pepper in the house." However, they insisted that I must provide them pepper for their soup. I explained it to them again with clarity that we don't have pepper in the house and the commander said to me "You boy, it is now 10:30am, I give you from now to 11:30am. If you do not provide the pepper we are requesting, we will kill you and cook your heart with this human heart." Once he said that, he fired the gun in our house 3 times then they left.

After they left, I decided to go from house to house in the neighborhood to ask for pepper, but nobody gave me any. Every house I entered they told me they had gone out of everything as well. One of the rebels came back and told me that what their commander has said to me is serious. I should not take it for granted. He said to me "If you won't provide that pepper, they will surely kill you." He asked me if I would like him to escort me to go on our farm to bring pepper before they kill me. I never hesitated, I quickly let him escort me to our farm to get some pepper.

He walked in front of me and I followed closely behind him to make it appear as much as possible that there was only one person walking until we could pass back by the check point to get on the main road. This was a great distance away from their checkpoint gate. Afterward, he left me alone to go on the farm. When I got on the farm, I quickly collected the pepper and wrapped it in the banana leaf and decided to go back into town, but before I could leave, when I lifted my head in the air, I could see a dark smoke going up in the air from the nearby village. I did not know what was happening in that village, all I knew was nobody was in that village at all because the rebels had also collected everyone from there as well.

I decided to quickly run and get back in the town where I came from. While I was running going back in the town where I had come from, the rebels there had gotten information that it was their enemy rebel group who was burning that town. So, their commander sent a whole troop to set an ambush the same way I was coming from and they did not know that I had gone back on the farm to get pepper. I ran from the farm until I got to the place where these solders were in the ambush. They initially saw me like one of the rebels that were burning the town, but others recognized me quickly from the distance and they made a sound to one another letting each other know I am one of the town boys that had been with them.

After their commander had recognized me, he sent one of the soldiers to quickly come and stop me from passing. When I saw the man that came out of the bush, I got so afraid because I did not know that they were in the bush. I started to explain myself to him why I went in the bush, but he kept stopping me from talking with a sign of quiet. He told me to follow him in the bush where their commander was, but I did not know why he wanted me to follow him in the bush. I decided to take a step back because I was so afraid, but he gave me the last warning to follow him otherwise he was going to shoot me, I bravely walked with him in the bush.

We finally reached the commander and he asked me so many questions: Where was I coming from? Who are those burning the town? How did I go back on the farm? Why did I go back on the farm? Out of all these questions, I was only able to answer two. Why I went back on the farm? and Who are those burning the town? My two answers were, I went in the bush because the commander asked me to provide pepper for them. Secondly, I did not know who was burning the town. He said to me, "Because you went in the bush without any of the soldiers knowing, he is giving the order for me to be killed."

He selected four of his men to take me to the town and execute me before he gets back from the bush. He sent me with his men and this specific instruction, "Before you get in the town with him, make sure to announce curfew hour." This meant everybody had to go indoors. They did exactly what he told them. Before we entered the town, they sent one person in the town to ask all the people to go indoors. At that moment, my parents did not know what was going on nor did anyone else in town.

They took me to the outskirts of the town and made me to stand under the papaya tree where they were going to kill me. When they put me under the papaya tree, they only had one heavy weapon with them called "German Machine Gun" (GMG) with five-gun shots in it. They could not use that gun to kill me because they had only a few shots reserved for an expected enemy attack. They instead asked one of their child soldiers, who was on the scene with a light weapon known as AK 47 gun, to use it so they could kill me. The child soldier refused. He told them his gun was to be used for enemies, it cannot be used to kill a civilian. While they were all arguing over which gun to use to kill me, their general advisor named *Good Finish,* who did not know what was going on, was coming from a farm with some of the town men. When he saw the group of soldiers standing under the papaya tree arguing, he came and asked, "What is going on here?" They told him this young man took a fire and carried it to the NPFL rebel to burn the nearby town.

This was a lie. As I made the attempt to explain to their advisor what was really going on, one of them slapped me hard to stop me from talking. They did not want me to tell him the truth. The advisor told them before he could say anything, the soldiers should go and keep me in jail until he could speak with the commander. So, they carried me and put me in jail.

While I was in jail, their general advisor who gave that order came in the jail to get information from me. I explained the actual story to him. He left and went to the general commander to ask for my release because what was said about me was not the actual story. The commander said he agrees to release me, but because I went back into the bush without anyone, he will lay me down and whip me twenty-five times. He ordered his bodyguard to lay me and whip me twenty-five times. After the whipping, my clothes were all soaked with blood from my butt and back. He told me to get up, go home, and do not do it again.

FIRE ON MY HOUSE

While we were still under the control of
the Unimo K rebels, it was one morning at 4am
and the NPFL rebels attacked them in the town
while we were all sleeping in our various houses.
We wanted to come out to escape in the bush,
but the Unimo K rebels stopped everybody from
coming outside. They told everybody to stay
indoors while they fought the rebel. The NPFL
rebels who attacked them drove all of them from
the town. All of us were left in our houses with
the NPFL rebels outside. This rebel group, who
captured the town from the Unimo, started
burning all the houses with the people in them.

My parents and I were still in our house with
some family members, the rebels put the fire on
our house through my room window, my mother
took the bucket of water and put out the fire from
outside. The rebel realized that somebody had
just put out the fire from our house. One of the
rebel soldiers kicked the back door of our house
to forcibly open the door and called everybody to
come out. We all started coming outside per their

request. Before we came outside, some of us were trying to grab food, clothing, and other things. I was confused about what to take from the house and escape with. I decided to only take my GOOD NEWS BIBLE with me. Before I came out, my little sister's husband came out ahead of me. His backpack was packed with tobacco leaf. He usually wraps the tobacco in paper to smoke as a cigarette. When I was about to come out, the two soldiers who told us to come outside, told my brother-in-law to stop running but he continued to run with his tobacco backpack, so they shot him two times. He ran until he dropped at the outskirts of the town by the banana bush.

While that was going on, they told me not to come outside yet. I stood in the hallway until my brother-in-law was shot. Afterward, they told me to get outside. When I came outside, one of the rebels pointed the gun at me. At the time he pulled the trigger, his friend knocked the gun down in his hand and the gun fired a bullet right between my legs. The gun shot penetrated and tore my trouser but did not touch me. He told his friend I do not think this boy is a part of them. They told me to run in the bush, otherwise I would be killed by any of their men. I began to run toward the bush. While I was running, I met my brother-in-law lying down on the ground, he saw me, lifted his head, and said, "Daniel, they shot me." Immediately at that time, the rebels saw him lift his head and ran to him saying, "Oh! you have not died yet?" The rebel then shot him in his head three times right in front of me and he finally died.

During that moment, I passed by him slowly until I ran in the bush. I ran in the bush so far and lay there about 4 hours until the gun sounds ceased. I was in the bush very scared to come out. I then heard a loud voice in the air say, "Civilians who are in the bush please come out, the NPFL rebels have gone." When I came out from the bush and entered the town, I saw that many of the town boys had been killed along with my brother-in-law. It was a sad moment for me and my parents to see so many having been killed, especially my sister's husband. My parents and I decided to leave the town to go to Lofa County for refuge.

FOREST SURVIVAL

My parents and I traveled to St. Paul River to live in another county (Lofa) for refuge. We decided to go there because my mother's family originally came from there. When we crossed the St. Paul River, we settled in a village called Vannla. When we left to go there, my mother took her eighty-year-old disabled auntie who needed care with her. When we got there, all the church members had left the village and the church was without a pastor or leader. I decided to take over the church as an evangelist.

My parents and I stayed in the village for eight months. Within that period, we ran out of the food that we took with us, even the salt. We started digging yams out of the bush to eat as a daily food. Every three days I would go into the bush and dig enough yams that would last us for another three days. One Sunday morning, my mother told me that we were out of yams. I told my mother, after service I will go in the bush to dig for yams to last another three days. After the service, I left my parents and other family in the town and went in the bush to dig for yams.

While I was in the bush, the NPFL Rebels entered this village we had settled in and collected everybody to carry them back across the St. Paul River into Bong County. When they were about to leave, my mother told them I was still in the bush, but the commander said, "We are on a do or die mission." Therefore, he told her, he could do nothing about me being left in the bush. According to my mother, the commander said to her, "God will take care of your son or the animals will eat him." They took my mother's auntie and her husband from among the group and told them to stay behind to wait for me. When they left the village with my parents and the other family, a few of their rebels stayed behind with their commander. They then took my mother's auntie and her husband under the plum tree and killed them.

At that time, I was still in the bush without any knowledge of what had gone on in the village. I got through digging the yams and left to go into the village. When I entered the village, the whole place was quiet. I did not hear any sounds from a person or animal. I began to wonder what had happened to my people. I thought they may have gone to a different village. I started to travel from village to village looking for them or anyone that I can find to get information from, but every village I entered, nobody was there.

Since I could not find anyone in the whole area, I decided to come back into the village where we stayed. I was 15 years old at this time and expected my parents to come back the next day to look for me. I was there for a complete two days and nobody came for me. I began to think that maybe something has happened to my parents, since no one was coming to find me. I decided to leave the village and go on one of the farms where people usually make their rice. I wanted to get away because the village was so silent and fearful.

Before I left the village, I decided to cut some banana leaves to wrap my yam that I cooked and planned to take with me. I happened to walk under the same plum tree where they had killed my mother's auntie and her husband. I lifted my head and saw lots of ants and flies on the leaves under the plum tree. I decided to get closer to see why the ants and flies were there. I then saw the two dead bodies lying down in the grass under the plum tree. At first, I did not recognize whose bodies they were. I got so afraid and ran back in the house, but I wanted to know whose dead bodies they were. I bravely walked back there and noticed that they were my mother's auntie and her husband.

I sat down for a whole hour thinking if whether my parents were killed too. I took my machete and one match box and went to live on the farm. Living there on the farm for the first week was difficult for me. I wondered if I would ever see my parents again, but I could not get any answer in my head. While I was living there, I had plenty of food because every farm I traveled to had lots of red bananas and bags of rice that people left behind. I settled in and got comfortable with my life.

After a few months, the matches in the matchbox ran out. After setting my last fire with them, I was careful not to let that fire go out because I did not have anything else that I could create a fire with. I maintained the fire that I had every day and night even when I left going anywhere. I would make sure to look for dry wood to keep the fire until I came back. I spent one year and two months in that forest land without seeing another human being. I would wonder to myself each day what day of the week it was along with many other thoughts. The only creatures I would ever see during that time were wild animals, birds, and different kinds of bugs.

After spending a little over a year alone in the forest, early one morning at the hour of 4am while sleeping, my father and four other guys entered the place I was living. My father came in where I was sleeping. In that moment I called him three times, "Daddy, is this you?" He answered me, "Yes, it is me, my son." He just held me with both his hands crying for five minutes without saying any words. Then he asked me, "How have you been my son?" I said, "I been doing good with the help of God." I asked him, "Daddy, why did you and mother leave me?" He just hugged me and began to cry again. I started crying too.

Everybody that came with him, embraced me with deep happiness. We left that same morning and went to my hometown (Bong County). When my mother saw me, she was very amazed. She told me right away, "Because you survived among the wild animals your name will no longer be Kolibah, but your name is now DANIEL." This is how my name changed from the village voodoo leader to the name of the man in the Bible who survived the lions' den.

YES, TO LIVE OR NO, TO DIE

When the rebel activities were spread all over Liberia, it made it difficult for farmers to continue with their normal routine of farming to produce food for their family. Since there was a shortage of food in our village, my three friends and I left our village to travel to another village to buy food one Sunday morning. During this day, other rebel forces had attacked that village and captured some of the villagers while others ran away. We did not know what was going on and we entered the village without knowing that another rebel group was there. The whole village was extremely quiet.

At once, four rebel soldiers abruptly came from between the houses at the same time and put us under gun point. We were considered as an enemy to them. They kept us locked up for one day until they brought everyone who lived there back to the village from the farms. They took us to their office to collect information from us to see if we were part of any rebel group. We explained to them that we were not part of any rebel group, but civilians who had come there to buy some food from the villagers for our family.

They asked us to join them to fight the other rebel group, but we all explained that we cannot join them because we had to take care of our families. They continued to insist that we should join them or else we will die. At this time, all the villagers had come to see what was going to happen to us. They said, "We are going to ask each of you an individual question, either you say yes and live, or you say no and die." While we were standing in line bound with rope, they had one of their young men stand right before us with his hand in the gun trigger ready to shoot.

They began to ask the question. They asked the first man "Are you willing to join us to fight?" He said, "No, I don't want to join the rebel." They shot him dead. The whole crowd yelled with crying. They asked the second person, "Are you going to join us to fight?" He bravely answered no after seeing the first man die. They shot him and he died. There was now two men left standing there to answer the YES TO LIVE OR NO TO DIE question. At that time, my parents and other people from my village had heard about what was going on in the village and they came to watch the event. When they came, surprising to them, I was part of the group. My parents and family were all in the crowd watching and throwing signs to me to say yes. They asked the third person and he said yes. They put him in the truck to take him to the training base. When they finally reached me, nearly all the crowd was crying for me not to say no, because they never wanted me to be killed.

At that time, their commander who did not know what was going on was making his way among the crowd to see what was happening. They asked me the question, "Do you want to join us to fight? I did not respond because I did not know what to say at the time. They asked me again the second time. I took a deep breath and I said, "Yes, I can join you, but not while you are still a rebel." There was so much noise that the soldier did not hear my response and before I could repeat it for him, their commander appeared in the middle of the crowd where I was standing and said, "Hold on! What is happening here?" They explained the problem to him, that we were captured on the enemy line and still refused to join them to fight. He said to them, "Why did you not bring this case to me, but decided to take your own order? Why did you kill the boys without my knowledge?" He gave an order to put all of them in jail and for them to untie me. He told me to go home with my parents and do not join soldiers anywhere.

CHAPTER 3

Entering the City

WHEN I WAS IN the village, after the Liberia civil war ceased, many of our family was displaced in the various parts of Liberia. Some of them got established in their displaced homes and started to grow food. My cousin Monune, who was one of the sons of the senator in the Liberia government, was also displaced in Lofa County. Lofa County is a county in the northernmost part of Liberia. When the war displaced him, he got settled with the Belle tribe. He was in a town known as Belle Yelle. He grew more food from his farm work while living there.

At some point there was a cease fire and things were calming down in our country. When my cousin Monune came back to his hometown from the displaced home of Belle Yelle, he had left behind most of his belongings including the entire rice he had harvested. He asked me to go back to Belle Yelle in Lofa County where he had been a displaced refugee because he needed someone to clean and sell his rice. He then wanted me to buy him some gold from the money I received from rice sales and bring him back any remaining cash. He promised me that if I did that for him then he will carry me in the city (Monrovia) to send me to school. When I heard that, I was excited and immediately went to my parents and told them exactly what my cousin and I discussed.

I accepted it with gladness and left the next day on my way to Lofa County. I spent eight months in Lofa County cleaning his seed rice, selling it, and then buying gold with the money. After completing the work, I was able to get 220 grams of gold, $500 United States dollars, $5,000 Liberian dollars, and five bags of clean rice. During the process of cleaning the rice, one of my shoes was ruined and I was given another slipper to use by a lady. There I was returning with a miss matched pair of shoes. I was careful not to spend any of his money for shoes or other things because he was trusting me.

When I got to the St. Paul River, while trying to cross, I lost my miss-match slipper in the river and I had no choice but to walk barefooted until I got to my hometown in Beletandla. They told me that my cousin had gone to Gbarnga, the capital city of our county, where his father was residing as a senator. I carried those items and presented them to my cousin in Gbarnga City, Bong County. He accepted those items with real happiness. He appreciated me wholeheartedly and told me to wait for him. He said I would go with him to Monrovia in one week and he would process my school situation so I can start.

I was so happy after hearing him share his plan with me because it had been my dream to go to school in the city. Then I asked him if he can allow me to go back in the village for my belongings and he said yes. In the village I was also serving in the Lutheran church as youth president and I wanted to go give that position to somebody else. I left that same day and went back in the village to tell my family and the Lutheran church members goodbye. When I got in the village, I told my parents and the church that I was now going to live in the city to attend school. My parents and the church had a farewell party for me that night.

The next day the youth members and some of my Dad's family escorted me to the next village where a motor car could be found. Once we got to the main road, I hugged all of them goodbye. After I entered Gbarnga, I went straight to my cousin to let him know I was back from the village. This time he did not give me a good response. The next day he sent one of his brothers to tell me that he will not be able to take me into the city at this time because he did not have money to transport me. He said I should go back to the village until he gets some money and then he will send for me.

I asked him was his inability to transport me the only reason why he was not taking me, and he said yes. I was so discouraged and even began to cry. It would be so shameful for me to return to the village and tell my family and the church members I was not going to the city for school after all. I just could not think of going back after the party and goodbyes. I began to wonder how I can transport myself to the city. I left and went to a place called Phebe. It has the biggest hospital in Bong County. I went there to look for somebody who could help transport me into the city. I believed from my cousin this was the only problem keeping me from being able to go with him. I met one doctor who was going into Monrovia. I asked the doctor to take me into the city and he agreed.

He dropped me off in the commercial marketplace area of the city where I did not know anyone. I did not know where to go and spent the whole day standing by one store wondering if I could find someone I knew. At around 8pm, I went and slept under the big market hall near the warehouse. At 5am the next morning, people began coming into the warehouse to sell and pick up their goods. I found two of my cousins who came to pick up supplies from the warehouse as well. They were very amazed to see me in the city because no one expected me to be there. They asked me how I got there, and I told them the agreement that was made between my cousin Monue and I. I spent the whole day with them at the marketplace and at the end of the day, they and I went together to my uncle's house.

When my uncle saw me, he asked me why and how I came to the city. I told him my cousin Monue had agreed to send me to school, but since he did not have money to transport me to the city, I asked one doctor from Phebe who brought me. I spent one week there at my uncle's house until my cousin Monue came. My uncle sent for him and asked him if it is true that he agreed to bring me to the city. He told him we had no discussion about me coming to the city. He told my uncle that if I knew how to get to the city, I would also know how to go back to the village. He said he had no place for me because he canceled the plan he had.

I was now at my uncle's house without a plan to go to school in the city, but only to go back on the farm where I came from. I was there for two weeks looking for the means to go back to my parents in the village. When I found another cousin in Monrovia, I explained my situation to him, and he told me he knows where my father's brother lives and works. I asked him if he can please take me to his house or where he works and he took me to his workplace. When I met him, I explained to him my whole situation. He told me, "Don't worry, I will not let you go back on the farm." He also told me the only thing he could not promise is to send me to school because he did not have the means. He said to me that I will stay there with him. I was now with my uncle in the city, but I was not going to school. The only thing I was doing in the city was washing, cooking, and running errands for him.

MY CITY EDUCATION EXPERIENCE

Like I said, when I got to the city of Monrovia, my cousin Monue who originally promised to sponsor me for school, let me down.

It was my uncle Professor Moses Y. Yarkpawolo who took me in, let me live with him, and stay at his house while he went to work.

He was a principal at the St. Peter's Lutheran High School. He eventually began taking me with him to help him do some schoolwork at his office. He taught me how to use the copy machine in the school. I began to copy some schoolwork. I also helped to be a timekeeper and ring the bell for students to come back from their break. I was doing this work as a volunteer for the school. This continued for two years. I was still yearning to go to school during this time.

One day, the old man who was working as a janitor in the school asked me if I was interested in going to school and I answered yes. I told him I had no one to sponsor me to go. He asked me if I would be willing to work as a janitor to go to school. I told him yes, I would be willing. He took me to my uncle who was the principal and told him that he sees potential in me and would like for me to work with him as a janitor so I can go to school. My uncle told him it was not in his power to make that decision. The next day this older man took me again to the Senior Pastor of the St. Peter Lutheran Church, Joseph Allison. He talked to him to allow me to work with him as a janitor so that I can go to school. Pastor Joseph Allison discussed it with the school board, and they agreed to let me work as a janitor and go to school. At that moment, my position was changed from production man to janitor. I was now working as a janitor in the morning hours and going to school in the afternoon.

PROMOTION BY RESPECT

I was 10 years of age when I had started my kindergarten education in the village. Growing up in my village, children were trained by their parents to always show the utmost respect to the older generation. I was one of the most kind and respectful kids in our village. The village school lacked teaching materials. My primary education was not strong because promotion to the next grade was based on how respectful students were, not on how knowledgeable you were. Due to the respectful training I received by my parents, I was always promoted at the end of the academic school year.

When I reached the age of 13, the Liberian civil war had taken over the country and no school was operating. I had only completed the 6th grade at that time. I did not attend any school for many years to come until the war had calmed way down. When I finally came to go to school in Monrovia, I was already eighteen years old. I knew how to be extremely respectful but was lacking in basic educational skills. Even though I had been promoted to the 6th grade in the village, I was not qualified for the 6th grade class in the city. The way they promoted me in my village did not prepare me for school in the city.

When I decided to continue my education, I did not know what class to take for the first year. I decided to start in the 4th grade class with no confidence that I could make it. In that 4th grade class, I was the biggest and oldest student in the class. So many people referred to me as the 4th grade's grandfather. Despite being made fun of by the students, I put time into studying my lessons more than all my other life activities.

I believe I was the humblest student in the class. I humbled myself to all the students big or little. I created a habit of praying to God every morning before I went on campus. I was given promotion twice in every academic year until I reached the 9th grade. I believe this was because of my faithfulness and diligence in learning. When I got in the 9th grade, the lessons and my job began to get much harder. Since my job on campus began before my classes, I started sleeping in the storeroom of the school through the week and would go home on the weekend. When I got to senior high (10th grade), my fellow students started to ridicule me with words like, "I will be a garbage cleaner."

MY SECRET AND SHAME

I had two classmates who were like best friends from the 7th grade until 10th grade. We did everything together so we can successfully pass our classes at school. We would study, do assignments, and take our test together. During this whole time, there was one thing I wanted to make sure of. I did not want my close friends to know that I was working in the school as a janitor. I felt that if I let them know, they would cut off our friendship. I would always let all the students leave from the campus before I started my janitor work. One day these friends asked me what kind of work I was doing at the school. I told them I was working as an office boy for the principal.

My uncle was no longer principal at the school by this time. We had another person in this position. One day, the old man janitor came to work very drunk and this principal would not allow him to work. It just so happened, while I was sitting in my class with my friends, a little girl had left from her class to run to her big sister for help to go to the bathroom. While she was on her way, she defecated on the steps in front of the bathroom. Since the janitor had been sent home by the principal, there was nobody else to clean up the mess.

The principal came into my class and asked the teacher to excuse me for a moment. He said to me, "Daniel, we have a serious problem here.

One of our nursery students has defecated all over the step. We will need you to help us clean it quickly before the students come out for a break." At the time it was just five minutes left before students were scheduled to come out for lunch break. I began to quickly hurry and try to clean up the mess before students came out because I did not want my friends to see me doing such work.

As soon I started cleaning the poop, the bell rang for break. What an embarrassing situation that was for me on that day! When I heard the bell ringing for break, I wanted to leave the work undone and walk away from there, but the principal was standing right there with me as I was doing the job. This janitor job was the only means for me to pay for my high school education and sustain myself financially in the city. When the bell rang for break, my two best female friends decided to come out quickly to find me for lunch. They came out so we can go into the cafeteria to eat but unfortunately they saw me cleaning boo-boo. They said in a loud voice, "Daniel what are you doing? Is that

71

punishment work?" The principal responded to their question before I could answer. He said, "No, it is not punishment work, he is doing his job. This is his job at the school to get his education."

From that moment, my two best female friends decided not to ever interact with me in anything; no eating with me, studying with me, or sitting together in the classroom. That day was a sorry day for me. I did not go back to the class that day. I left and went behind the school building sitting there weeping so bitterly. I said I will never go back to the school anymore, nor will I work there as a janitor. I did not want my classmates to make even greater fun of me.

While I was crying, two of the schoolteachers came and met me. They asked me, why was I crying? After I explained the problem to them, they tried to comfort me, but I could not stop crying. They went and told the principal. He called me in his office and offered me a cold bottle of Coca-Cola. He gave me a word of encouragement. He said, "Daniel don't let shame take away the opportunity God has for you. This is not your future work. God will give you a better future tomorrow and those who are making fun of you will be proud of you tomorrow, so don't give up." After he spoke these words to me, I became so encouraged and was never ashamed of working in the school as a janitor again. Although some students made even more fun of me than ever before after that day, I never felt embarrassed. The more they made fun of me, the more diligent I was to study my lessons and make good grades.

STUDYING UNDER THE MOONLIGHT

When I got promoted to the tenth grade, the lessons became harder. I could not understand the various science courses. I was working in the school as a janitor Monday through Friday from 7am to 2pm. I was attending school Monday through Friday from 2pm to 5pm. I did not have adequate time to study my lessons. As a janitor in the school, I was constantly going in and out of the classroom to do janitorial work. This caused me to miss out on many of the teacher's explanations on my various subjects.

My classmates organized a group study class on a particular day to meet and study together. I decided to join and study with them. When I planned this, they had already planned to meet at Tubman High School on 12th Street in Sinkor. This was set up for every Saturday at 5pm. At that same time, the St. Peter's Lutheran School administration had decided to host their regular weekly meeting every Saturday at 5pm. It was mandatory for me to be in this school administration meeting every week because I was a janitor at the school.

Working as a janitor in the school was the only opportunity for me to attend school or pay my school fees. I was told by the school administration that if I did not attend the meeting, I could not continue to work in the school. I knew if I did not attend the student study class at the Tubman High School campus, I would not be able to understand my lessons. It was impossible for me to be at the two locations at the same time. What could I do? If I do not go to the school meeting, I will not have a job or continue schooling. If I do not go to the student's study, I will not pass in the school. I struggled with the decision of what to do for a whole week. I decided to not attend the student's group study and continue to focus on my job since it was the only means of finances to pay my school fees.

A big problem I faced was that I did not have enough money to buy candles so I could study in the evening. In Africa, the moon light can shine at night like real electricity. I decided to study under the moonlight at night. I waited until everybody went to bed in the city, then I would come outside to study using the moon light. In Liberia, the climate is tropical and hot because of the high level of water vapor in the atmosphere. The heat outside would always force me to take off my clothes and wear only a tank-top shirt and boxer shorts while I studied. I did an outside midnight study four months during my 10th grade year and my grades improved. I continued this study process, studying under the moon light, until I graduated from high school.

FOOD ISSUE

The St. Peter's Lutheran School always provided food for the students. This food was always cooked by a few women and distributed in every classroom. The food was brought in a big dig pan with spoons and plates. Every student served themselves from the big dig pan. Each time they brought my class food, everybody would go to get their food from the dig pan, but when I went to get my food, the other students would not want to eat any of that food anymore. The reason they were doing this was because I was working as a janitor in the school. They never wanted me to eat with them from the same pan. I did not know that this was what was going on, nor did the school administration know either. After two weeks, a friend of mind called me and said that the students were refusing the food because of me.

He explained to me that the students did not want to eat with me because I worked there as a janitor. My work included cleaning bathrooms and I should not eat out of the same pan they eat out of. When I heard about this embarrassment caused by me in the school, I went to enquire about the possibility of getting my food separately.

I went in the kitchen, where the food was being prepared, and talked to the women that were responsible to cook the food. I asked them if they could possibly keep food for me. They agreed to keep food for me every day they cooked. So, my food was now separated from my fellow students. I was able to get my student food every day directly from the cooks. I went through all these difficult struggles but did not give up. In my life I have had to fight and always was able to move ahead because I believed when the Bible said,

> **"THE RACE IS NOT TO THE SWIFT OR STRONG BUT TO THOSE WHO ENDURE TO THE END."**

I have always been a dreamer and believer that I will fulfill everything God has put in me to do on earth. As Nelson Mandela said and I quote,

> "A winner is a dreamer who never gives up. Education is the most powerful weapon which you can use to change the world."

CHAPTER 4

Overcoming Temptation

I WORKED AS A JANITOR at St. Peter's Lutheran High School while attending the same school to obtain my high school diploma. When I graduated from high school, the Lutheran administration decided to send me to the financial office to work with the accountant and cashier. My job title was expeditor. There were many temptations and trials that came my way while working in the financial office with the cashier as an expeditor. My first year in the financial office, there was a serious burglary that took place. We had $95,000 Liberian dollars stolen from the financial office after only my second month working there.

The administration looked at me as a potential suspect since for so many years that had never happened in the school.

I was arrested and put in jail for three days while the police were investigating. During those three days in jail, the police caught the four students that committed the act. The school administration tested me all kind of ways before assigning me to the financial office. I also went through other testing. I will share some of those tests.

FINAL EXAM FRAUD

One Thursday night, I had slept with hunger and went to work Friday morning with no money in my pocket to buy food. When I got to the school, the principal told me to help arrange the final exam test papers for all the students. The principal and school registrar left me in charge and went home for the day. While arranging the test papers by classes in the production room, four senior students walked on the campus. They saw me arranging the test papers and showed me a United States one-hundred-dollar bill. They offered me the money if I would give them each a copy of all the 11th and 12th graders test. Even though I was hungry with no money to buy food for the next week, I refused to leak the instructor's tests. I refused to accept the money because I knew it was not God's will and it was not going to help them in their futures.

CASH IN TRASH

The cashier tried me with all kinds of test to determine if I was a person of integrity. One day she put $200 in Liberian bills in the trash can in the bathroom and asked me to clean the bathroom before going home. When I went to clean the bathroom, I felt she mistakenly dropped the money in the trash can. I took it and kept it in the drawer. The next morning when I came to work, I told her I saw money in the trash can and put it in the drawer. She said, "Oh thank you. I lost that money, but I am glad you found it for me."

After a few weeks she dropped a $500 dollar bundle on the floor in the office and left for home. I saw the money on the floor when cleaning the office, I took it and safely kept it in the drawer. The next morning, I said, "Boss lady, you mistakenly left some money again on the floor." She said, "Thank you very much Daniel, I did not even think of it."

One day she told me, "Since you live in town near the bank, you will always carry the daily money collection with you home." In the morning I was to carry it to the bank before coming to work. Each day she always gave me twenty-five to thirty thousand Liberian dollars to take home and carry to the bank in the morning before I arrived at work. I did that for several months without any complaints.

ESCAPE AND PAY LATER

When the Liberian Civil War ended, the United Nations decided to take the guns from those rebels and put them in school to learn a trade for themselves instead of fighting. They decided to give a certain amount monthly for each ex-rebel going to school. The money was sent to most schools in Monrovia as allowances for those former rebels. St. Peter's Lutheran was given a certain amount as well. There came a time for the school to pay these ex-fighters their allowances. My boss lady sent me to the bank for the money. The total amount of money was $85,000 United States dollars.

When I received the money, I sat in the bank and called a taxi driver to take me to the school. A friend of mind came in the bank and saw me with the money. He asked me did the people really trust me with this money. I said yes. Then he said to me, "My friend, this is an opportunity for you to go in any western world. This world is not fair and will never be fair until the judgment day comes. Before you get rich in this world, you have to do something." He said to me "If you leave this country and go to any developed country it will only take you a few years to pay back the money, but you will now be established." He tempted me with his smooth talk, but all he said did not move me. I knew

God had more opportunities for me than that, so I refused to follow his evil plan. I continued to wait for the taxi driver to come and take me on the campus.

LIBERIA REVENUE OFFICE

In 2004, the St Peter's Lutheran School was audited by the Liberian Revenue office. They received a notice that the school owed the Liberian government for twelve years of taxes. When the government realized that the school had not been paying taxes, the Liberian Finance office fined the school $12,000 United States dollars including interest and penalty. One morning when I went to work, my boss lady gave me the $12,000 in cash to go and pay it to the Liberian Ministry of Finance. I was instructed to deposit the money into Liberian Revenue account at the bank. I only needed to get a bank deposit slip from the Ministry of Finance office to fill out and proceed to the bank. I went to the office to get the deposit slip first.

When I got there with the money, the minister of the revenue department saw me with this money. He asked, "What are you doing here?" I told him I came to pay the St Peter's Lutheran School taxes. He called me in his office and offered me a cold bottle of Coca-Cola. He asked me, "Is this the tax fine payment that we put on St. Peter Lutheran?" I said yes. He then said okay. He told me he was going to make sure to have it under control in his power as a minister of Liberia in the Revenue Department. Then he tried to convince me to give him the money so he can give me a (false) receipt to take it to the school as if the money has been paid. I said no. I must take this money to the bank because if the people do not see this payment in the bank they will come after me. He said to me, "My friend, I am the boss in this whole department. It is me who imposed the fine on them and it is me that can revoke it with no trouble." He guaranteed me there is no need to worry. He wanted to give me $1000 of this money and a clean flag receipt (legitimate) for it. He said the receipt will have no trouble at any time. I told him I will not do that. The only thing I can do is take the money back to the school and have another person do that transaction with you. He backed off. I finally received a slip from his office and deposited the money into the bank account as instructed.

MONEY FOUND IN BANK

When I was working with St. Peter Lutheran School, my school tuition and fees were paid through my salary. At graduation I still owed a balance of $28,000 Liberian dollars. After I graduated and my high school loan was paid off, I was now getting my whole paycheck of $6000 Liberian dollars which was about $50 United States dollars per month. I took my first pay to the Liberian Bank Development Investment (LBDI) to open a savings account.

When I arrived and went to the counter of the customer deposit slip filling station, there was a red bag laying on the table with no one around. When I opened this red plastic bag, it had $6,000 United States dollars in it. I took this money bag and put it in my backpack and went to stand in the line to deposit my $6000 Liberian dollars. While I was standing in line to open my savings account, the devil brought all kind of thoughts to my mind. The thought came to leave the bank with this money and never open the savings. Another thought came to open the savings account and put this money in it as my personal money. The final thought was to wait to see if anyone will come and ask for this money.

I decided to ask people if they had lost a bag. No one could tell me they misplaced a bag. I left and went to the bank president's office and reported a bag lost and found. The bank president could not believe that I found such money in the bank and reported it. She told me to stay in her office until she found out who owned the money. She wanted to make sure we found the rightful owner.

We would soon find out it was left there by the accountant from the pharmacy Sonia's. He had gone to the bank to make the weekly deposit from his workplace. This accountant filled in the bank deposit slip over the counter and left the bag of money laying on the counter. He stepped out to take a phone call and handle his own business without realizing he did not have the money with him. It took 30 minutes, for this gentleman to realize he misplaced the money. He started to look for the money in secret because he did not want anybody to know that he had misplaced a bag of money.

He called his job to find out if he had left it there, but they told him the money was not there. He went to the restaurant where he stopped first that morning for breakfast. They told him there was no bag left there either.

By the time the accountant who lost the money bag had went to one of the bank managers to report his money lost, the bank manager had already received directions from the bank president. I had already spoken to her about the found bag and she had notified the bankers to find out if somebody had lost a money bag. She gave a strict order to them that if anyone had lost a money bag, the person should describe the bag and how much money was in the bag.

When the accountant reported to the bank manager that his bag was missing, the manager asked him the security questions about the lost item. He asked him what the bag color was and the amount in the bag. Every question was answered correctly. When all the information was correct, the president of the bank took me in front of her workers and presented the money to the accountant and gave me a great compliment of being an honest customer. The man who lost the money was relieved. He said he thought the money was in his backpack. He really appreciated my help. He gave me $25 U.S. dollars from his own pocket. After many people heard about it, most of them referred to me as the most stupid Kpelle man from Bong County.

OVERPAYMENT AT BANK

After my first year in the United States, I was always home because I did not get any job yet. My host was always working from 7am to 4pm. Since I was always home because I was not working, he would call me to come to his job to collect our rent so I can make a payment at the office. One day I went to collect the rent from him to make the payment at the apartment office. When I went there, he had not gone to the bank to get the money. He took me to the bank to get the money, but when we arrived in the bank it was crowded. He could not stay to get the money because he had to go back to work. He spoke with a bank representative to authorize me to get $1,000 dollars out with his identification.

I stood waiting in line for a teller so I could get this money. When it was finally my turn to be helped by the teller, she told the rest of the people standing behind me that I was the last customer she would help. She had the security to close the line behind me. When I got to her window, she wanted to send me to the next window, but every window was crowded and busy. She decided to service me very quickly. She realized immediately that my transaction was not from my own account, but my host and her boss had worked it out and he came over to approve this transaction. She hurriedly processed the $1000 dollars withdraw. She asked me how I wanted my cash and I said give me everything in tens. After I signed for the withdrawal, she mistakenly took one bundle of 100's and handed it to me. She said thank you for coming, closed her window, and put up a next window sign.

When I realized she had just handed me $10,000 dollars, I took a step back and begin to wonder about what she just did. I asked myself did she do it intentionally or by mistake. I put the money in my pocket and sat down in the customer waiting area to think. Many thoughts came into my mind. Should I carry the money and tell my host, who left me there, what happened? I canceled that thought. I then thought of carrying the money and giving only one thousand dollars to my host and keeping the rest for myself. I cancelled that thought also. I begin to think about the Word of God in Galatians 6:9 that says, "We should not get weary in doing good."

I said to myself, I am not carrying this money. I am going to return it to the lady and say you made a mistake and overpaid me. I went back to the window to try to speak to her, but the man said she was busy, and he could help me instead, if I needed any help. Since I did not want for any of her bosses to know that she had made a mistake, I said I wanted to speak to her directly. They went and told her, but she said she was not coming I can get help from any of the bank workers. So, I was left with no other option but to explain to the man that she made a mistake and gave me $10,000 instead of $1,000.

The man quickly opened the booth and let me in. He went to the lady and told her why I wanted to see her. She left everything and ran to me in the office. I showed her the money she gave me. She said Oh! Thank you! She took the $100 bundle from me and gave me the $10 bundle. She wanted to give me $20 dollars from her pocket as a kind gesture, but I said it was okay. I told her, "I did not do it for pay, I only wanted to be honest." I left and went home.

In the evening when my host came from work, I told him what happened to me in the bank. He said, "Daniel, are you crazy? Why would you give that money back? Don't you know it was a blessing God gave to you to start your life in the U.S. with?" I said, "It was not a blessing. If I had taken that money, the lady could have been fired from her job and responsible to pay the money back."

CHAPTER 5

U.S. Embassy Greystone War

IN 2003, THREE REBEL forces attacked Monrovia (capital city of Liberia) and many residents that were living in central Monrovia were forced to live together in one community called Buzzy Quarter. There was no food in this community. The only area food could be found was at the Capital City Business Center known as Waterside. Waterside was close to a community in Monrovia called West-Point. It was the war zone which the three rebel forces were fighting to capture. The head of every household that resided in the Buzzy Quarter community had to find their way to Waterside to get food for their family. Families would sell some of the food they brought from the Waterside to others who would not risk their lives. The cost was high. Many men and women were being killed by stray bullets from the rebel zone each day. I was always afraid to go to the Waterside for food because of the daily deaths that occurred. One day my friend was going to buy some food for his family in Waterside, so I decided to go with him to get some food for my family too. We planned to leave Tuesday morning because most of the attacks always took place in the afternoon. While we had planned to go to Waterside that morning, another rebel group decided to attack Waterside that same morning and of course we knew nothing about it.

We had already decided to pass the back way by the U.S. Embassy in Libera to go to Waterside. While we were on our way at 7am, rebel soldiers were already deployed in the zone where we were headed to get food. When we got to the area of the American Embassy called Greystone, just 5 minutes away from Waterside, some rebel groups opened fire on each other. Many bullets were flying from the place we came from, which was now too dangerous for us to pass back again. Rebels were ahead of us shooting guns and stray bullets were flying behind us. Both of us decided to bravely return, but neither one of us wanted to be in front of the other one.

We stood there for 5 minutes wondering which way to go but we could not find any safe way to go. I thought of the Bible verse that says, "For everyone who calls on the name of the Lord will be saved." (Roman 10:13) I decided to call on the name of the Lord for mercy in a loud voice while going the way we initially came from. My friend kept telling me to keep quiet, but I could not keep my mouth shut from asking God for help in a loud voice. My friend said he will go a different way if I did not stop making noise, but I could not stop calling on the name of Jesus for help. So, he took a different route to go because I would not stop asking God for help. After he left me, I continued praising God and asking for His mercy and safety while returning home on the same route we had come from.

When I got to the intersection, I saw one of the NPFL rebel soldiers. He stopped me and

I stood there until he made sure that everywhere was safe for me to cross the road. Then he called me to cross and walk fast to go home because somebody had been hit by a stray bullet and died. When I got to the spot, I realized that it was my friend who was hit by the bullet. While my friend was running home, he had come to the intersection to cross the road to get to the other side where the Buzzy Quarter community we were all living at was. Before he could make the attempt, he was hit by a stray bullet from rebel gun fire and died instantly. I started to run until I got into the Buzzy Quarter community. Many people came asking me if I brought food to sell. I told them I was not able to reach the Waterside market because there were too many gun sounds all around us, so we decided to come back. I continued to say, "While coming back, my friend took a different way to come home and unfortunately got hit by a stray bullet and died instantly."

A larger crowd came around me to find out what happened. I told them I knew we were in the danger zone coming back home and I asked

God to cover us with safety. I explained to them how my friend said I was making noise, so he took his own route away from me. One of the community leaders later came and told the people, "This is a sign that we will not be safe in our own way." He told them that the young man who died was hiding from God. He was finding his own safety on the way home.

CHAPTER 6

Coming to the United States

GROWING UP AS A little boy, I had always wanted to travel to the United States. Therefore, I decided that I would live my life in a way where nothing could hinder me from going. In my Liberia tribe, there was a belief system that said, "If a person dips bread in tea and then eats it, they could never go to America." Every morning my mother would always fix our breakfast and cut a slice of bread for everyone with a cup of tea. I would never dip my bread in the tea while eating because of this superstition. Although this belief has no proof, I still would never dip my bread into my tea because I thought it might keep me from going to America.

I heard about the Immigrant Diversity Visa Program that America has for countries around the world. This program from the U.S. Government gave people an opportunity to travel to the United States. I decided to apply for this program. I first applied in the year 2000 before my high school graduation. The results came back in 2001 and I was not selected. In the following year of 2002, I played this DV program again and when the results came in 2003, I did not find my name again. After that, I lost hope in the DV program. I said to myself, if I go to America, it will not be through this program, so I am not going to spend my money to play again. It was like playing the lottery. It cost me $300 Liberian dollars each time I played.

After my graduation I started praying to God for open opportunities to travel to the United States. I saw no sign of any opportunity until 2005. In 2005, there was another season for the DV program. I did not play until the second to last week in that year before the DV program was set to end. At the time I decided to play, I did not have money during that week. On the last available day to play the 2005 DV program, that morning a radio announcement from the American Embassy aired saying it would end at 6pm. I still did not have anywhere to get money to play.

That day I was very hungry in the morning and I decided to walk to my friend's workplace. He worked at the movie theater. I asked him to buy me some food to eat. While I was walking on the sidewalk, a government car passed by me speeding. I saw a $20 United States bill fly from this car and land right under my feet. I picked up this money and stood there for 30 minutes waiting to see if this car would come back for this money, but no one came back. I took this money and decided to go and play the DV program before the time expired. I was thinking to myself, "What if I play this DV program and don't win again?" I went to downtown Monrovia and played at the internet café hoping God would let me win this time.

All who had played that year, waited for the results to come November 2006. I was feeling very reluctant to go and check for my name. I said to myself, "I don't think I even made it this time, so I am not wasting my time to go there." The result was still up for two months. Some of the students from the school I graduated from, asked me, "Daniel, did you play the DV program last year?" I said, "Yes, I did." They told me, "We saw your name up." I did not believe it because the students were always playing funny games with me, so I did not bother to go there.

The following week another person came and told me again, "Daniel we saw your name on the DV results board as a winner." The next day I went there and saw my name. I was happy, but still did not want to get my hopes up too much because wining the DV does not guarantee you coming to the United States unless you meet all the requirements. They sent me a packet that had all the information I needed to know on documentations I would need to submit before they scheduled me for an interview.

I put all this information together and sent it to the American Embassy. It took them six months to post the names for those who were qualified for an interview. I went to the American

Embassy and I saw my name was up for an interview. I was so happy. I did not even know what to do. All the qualified candidate's names were written on a wide large bulletin. There was lots of information after each name right before their interview date. I followed the line with my finger to the very end to see when my interview date was. While I was following the line, I missed my line and copied another person's interview date leaving with great excitement.

I did not return there until that interview day. When I went to the American Embassy on that day, I was waiting for my name to be called. I waited for the whole day until they were about to close, and my name was not called. I asked one of the employees to ask the consular why my name was not called. They checked the listing from start to end and did not see my name. They told me your name is not on the list. I became so confused and did not know what to do. I showed them all the documents that proved I was one of the DV candidates for that year. They told me, "But your name is not on the list."

I was hungry so I left and went to buy some food from a food vendor who was selling right outside the embassy. The food was very tasteless because I did not have any appetite after what I heard at my visa interview. While I was eating, I heard someone calling my name in a loud voice, "Daniel Sumo." It was the security guard calling me and stating someone in the embassy office was looking for me. I went in and they told me that I missed my interview date three months ago. I asked, "What can I do now? They said nothing because the head consular official had left for the United States and the DV program was over that same day. I would need to try again another year.

I left the embassy very sad. My plans ended again unsuccessfully. I thought about ending my life. I thought about leaving the country for another one. Lastly, I thought I would just go back in the village and live with my parents to be a farmer. I was ashamed to go back to my community during the day because I did not know what to tell people who would ask me what happened. I went to a community market and sat there until the evening before going home. When I arrived home that night, I was so ashamed I did not even let anyone know I was there. I did not sleep at all that night.

I continued to pray for the whole night until the next day. I left and went back to the embassy the next day to talk to the authority to consider me. When I got there, one of the consular told me if I continued to hang around the embassy, she will call the police on me. She reminded me that the DV program is over and I have been denied so there is nothing they can do about my case. I left the embassy and went back to my job to talk to my boss and see if he can allow me to get my job back since they denied my visa. My boss man told me they had filled my position with another person already. I felt sad and depressed more than even before. I left with no hope, no plan, and no direction in my life. I decided to pray to God for help. I began to fast for five days. During this fast, I ate nothing and only drunk water. I talked to God more than talking to people. I kept myself indoors to hear from God. I did this for five days praying day and night and it seemed like nothing was happening.

At the end of five days was a Friday, and I received a call from a white lady. She told me she was calling from Kentucky in the United States. All I heard was, I am a king calling from the United Nations. I repeated this and she said no. I said, "Go ahead. I am listening." She said a visa is coming for you from Kentucky in the United States. I did not hear the communication clear, but I heard visa is coming for you. So, I asked her three times, "Where can I get this visa?" She could not really understand me but said it will arrive at the U.S. Embassy in Monrovia. She hung up. I now had some hope. I still do not know to this day who this lady is and how she received my phone number and information. I decided to get rid of all those negative thoughts in my mind. I began to praise God for answering my prayer, but I decided not to tell anybody until my blessing came true.

After the weekend, I waited for a call from the U.S. Embassy and I did not get a call from them. I decided to go there and tell them about the call. Something in my mind said do not go there because the person that called you did not say go there or call the Embassy. She said the Embassy will call you. So, I decided to wait and keep trusting God. Monday, Tuesday, and Wednesday went by and I did not receive a call from the Embassy. On Thursday I received a call to go to the Embassy at 11am. I decided to get there early. I went to the Embassy at 9:30am that day and waited for 11am. At 11am they called me in and asked if I ever called anybody from the United States for a visa. I told them no, somebody called me. They said a visa was sent for you from Kentucky in the United States. They handed me the visa and welcomed me to the United States.

VISA TO GO

My visa was about to expire because I did not have the money to buy the expensive plane ticket. The visa given to me had a six-month expiration date that could not be re-issued. If I did not leave to the United States before this expiration date, I would not be able to travel. At the time the visa was issued to me, my plane ticket to the United Sates was $1,400 United States dollars. I did not have this type of money, nor did I know how I would get it.

I decided to visit and ask all my uncles for assistance who were working with the government in Monrovia. Each one of them told me they did not have money to help me. I went to my parents in the village to ask them if they can get money from anyone to help me. My dad told me that they only had $1,500 Liberian dollars to help me. This was equivalent to $15 United States dollars. I left and went back to Monrovia to seek help from friends, but I could not get any assistance from anyone. I went to my former job to ask them for a loan, but they would not help me.

Lastly, I decided to write a letter to government officials in my effort to get assistance. I wrote a few senators and did not receive help from any of them. This whole process continued for just over five months. I was down to only three weeks left to travel or be stuck in Liberia with an expired visa. I was in desperate need with no one to help me. I went home, put the visa down, and prayed to God for help. I spent one whole day at home praying to God for help. The very next day, I received a call from the accountant lady who was my supervisor when I worked at the Lutheran school. She wanted me to come to her house. When I got to her house, she took me in her room and said to me, "Daniel you have been a faithful boy working with me, therefore I cannot let your visa expire because you don't have the money to buy your plane ticket." She gave me $1,500 United States dollars to buy the plane ticket to travel to the United States. This is how God blessed me so I could purchase my plane ticket.

CHAPTER 7

My American Dream

I REMEMBER WHEN I BOUGHT my plane ticket to travel to America, I felt all the stress from financial and family burdens leave my body. I was thinking I was no longer a failure but a success; no longer going to be poor but rich. When the Brussels plane arrived at the Roberts International Airport in Liberia, it felt like cool air was blowing on me with a sweet taste in my mouth. When I got on the plane, I lifted both my hands and began to glorify God for taking away my suffering, disgrace, stress, and failure in life. I thought to myself there were no poor men in America. America was a place where everyone who goes there becomes rich.

This was my first time entering and riding on a plane. When I came on the plane, I did not know what to do or how to select my seat. I went straight to the VIP area and sat in one of those seats close to the pilot. I thought you could sit in any available seat. As I was getting comfortable in this seat, one of the airline attendants asked me, "Are you supposed to be sitting here?" I said, "Yes, because nobody was here, and I was the first to sit here." She said, "Let me see your boarding pass." After she saw my boarding pass, she told me that my seat was at the back. She took me to my window seat on the very last row in the back of the plane. She asked me several questions. Are you traveling with someone? I said, "No." She said, "Have you ever traveled before?" I said, "No." She said, "Do you need any further help?" I said, "No, I got it." She left me alone.

When we landed in Amsterdam, I needed to transfer to United Airlines. I did not know I did not need to collect my luggage because I would collect them at my last destination in San Francisco. So, when I got off the Brussels plane, I went out to the baggage claim area to collect my luggage. I stood there watching everyone's luggage coming but did not see mine. I left and went to ask one of the airport workers. The person I asked looked at my boarding pass. She told me that I am not supposed to collect my bags. She directed me to my next boarding area. When I arrived, they told me my plane had left. I had just missed my next flight.

The United Airlines agent put me on another plane to San Francisco Airport which would leave in another two hours. When I left Amsterdam Airport, I arrived at San Francisco Airport at 7pm instead of 3pm as originally scheduled. The first person that talked to me was a dirty homeless man who was asking me for 25 cents. I was shocked and confused. Disappointed, I asked myself, "Is this really the USA?" I asked my family who came to pick me up from the airport about the homeless man asking me for money. I wanted to know if this was real. My cousin looked at me and said, "My brother you haven't seen anything yet, wait until you get to the city of Oakland. You will see many of those people begging you for your leftover food." When

I heard this, I was even more confused about my expectation of the United States of America.

GETTING STARTED

When I arrived in the United States, I went to Pittsburg, California to live with family until I received my documents issued to me from the State of California. When I arrived at my family's house, I was welcomed with gladness. I was given a special room in the house. After three days in the United States, my cousin kindly explained to me that since his mother is in the house with them and there are only two rooms in the apartment, I will need to sleep in the living room on the sofa until I can get a job.

I slept on the living room couch for 6 months until I got all my documentation. After I got my documentation, I started to look for a job. I put in many applications online, but still did not receive any calls. I decided to visit some of the places I applied to inquire about my application status. I was told at these places that they needed somebody who had 6 to 12 months of experience. Being a newcomer to the USA, I did not have any job experience here. One year went by without me finding a job.

There was a Christian American lady who took me into another city to do yardwork for one of her friends for monthly pay. When I arrived at this lady's house, she showed me her yard and agreed to pay me $700 per month. She said to me because they had foster children living with them, I could never sleep in the house. She offered me her old camper van parked outside to sleep in as needed. After spending the first month there, she said she will keep my money in her bank account until I was ready to go home.

She allowed me to use her house phone to call family in Liberia and Pittsburg. I was sleeping in that camper van while working in the yard. The lady's husband told me he does not want to see me in his house except when I needed to clean the living room floor. The lady told me to come clean the living room after her husband left the house. So, I would always wait until the man left the house, then his wife would call me quickly to come and clean the living room in a hurry before her husband came home. After cleaning the house, she would always let me use her house phone to call my family in Liberia and Pittsburg. One day I was cleaning the living room and the man abruptly came home. He met me cleaning the living room floor and was really annoyed with his wife. He wanted me out of his house. He yelled at me in a loud voice, "Hurry up and get out of my house you stupid fool." I quickly hurried up cleaning and left his house.

I spent 6 months working for them, but I did not see a paycheck one day. I received none of the cash I had worked for. I did not have control over my own money I worked for and during any mealtime I was the last to eat. It got to a point I felt that I had not been treated well working for them. I told the lady that I was ready to leave. She said to me that I can leave, but she cannot give me my money because when I was there, I was using her phone to call my family in Liberia and Pittsburgh. She showed me her phone bill with all the charges from my Liberia calls. Her phone bill was $2,000 United States dollars. Because of this, I left her place without any money.

When I returned to my family's house, I realized that the grace period they had for me to live with them without paying rent had expired. My host said, "We will consider you for this month without the rent payment but next month you must pay a portion of the rent." I struggled to tell him I would, even though I did not have money or a job. The next day I was on the bus to the career center to apply for a job. I applied for multiple jobs but all of them were asking for at least 6 months to a year experience once again. I went to the career center everyday but could not get any job.

One day I decided to stop going to the career center and go to some of these job places and start declaring victory. I walked from our apartment complex to Burlington Coat Factory store where I applied first. I began to declare job offer victory during my walk. When I entered the store, I felt afraid to ask for the manager, so I just acted like an ordinary customer. I went back home without any results from the store. After I went back to my family's house, the phone rung and my auntie picked it up and the call was for me from the same Burlington Coat Factory I had just left. They were calling me with a job offer. I was offered a job to work in the receiving with no job experience. I worked there for 6 months and got fired by the manager because she said that many people could not understand my English.

Now I was qualified to apply for unemployment because I had worked in the United States for at least 6 months. I received unemployment benefits while going to Certified Nursing Assistant school until I graduated from the Advanced Medical School of Nursing. After I graduated, I got my first nursing assistant job with the Antioch Convalescent Hospital. I was now able to pay a portion of my house rent in my family's house while still sleeping in the living room.

MY ROOMMATE'S DEATH

As time went on, I was asked to leave from my residence in Pittsburgh, California. I left and rented a bedroom in Antioch, California. Within three months, I was kicked off my job again because the manager could not understand my English. I could not afford to pay my rent anymore. My landlord gave me a one month notice to leave for no rent payment. Immediately, I was offered a one bedroom in Oakland, California by a church organization to share a place with the associate pastor. The associate pastor and I lived together as roommates for a year and a half. One morning, my car got stolen from the parking garage. I no longer had a car to go places.

One day I received a call from my mother in Liberia. When I responded to the call she said, "Son call me back quickly and let me tell you something serious." I did not have a calling card or any international credit on my phone to call my mother back. At that time, it was now 7:30pm which was the time my roommate usually arrived home. I called my roommate and asked him if he can take me to the store to buy a calling card to call my mom when he arrived home. He said to me, "Where are you?" I replied, "I am at home." Then he told me to come wait for him on the road. He said "I am driving home. I have two ladies in my car that I am taking home. I will pick you up when I drop them off, then I can take you to the store to buy your calling card."

Immediately I left the house and went on the road to wait for him. Two minutes later he pulls up in front of the apartment home. Before I went to get in his car, I realized that I did not have my phone with me. I said, "Oh! I forgot about my phone in the house." He said, "Let's go Daniel! When we come back you can make the call in the house." I said, "No, I need to get my phone." He let me go in the house to grab my phone quickly. After I came out of the house to get in the car, I realized he left without me. He was already gone.

I felt so bad and decided I would never ask him for any assistance anymore. I called him but he did not answer his phone. I said to myself, when he comes back, I will express my feelings to him about what he just did to me. I went back in the house to wait for him. I waited for him a long time, but he never returned. Since he took so long to come back, I assumed that he had probably slept over at someone else's place.

I went to bed for a good night sleep. In the morning when I got up, I went to check in his room, but he was not in. I called his phone, and it went to voicemail. I decided to turn on the television to watch some morning news. The news reported that a car had crashed on a certain road and killed a 52-year-old African man last night. I came out and ran to the road, which was not far from where I lived to find out who that African man was. When I got there, I heard that a policeman was chasing the car of an armed robber. The armed robber's sport utility vehicle (SUV) crashed into my roommate's car and smashed it to the ground as he was coming on that road.

God delivered me. I was supposed to be in that car. When my roommate left me, I saw it as a bad thing, but it was God's divine favor on my life. I began to wonder if I had been in the car with my roommate, after he dropped those women off, we both were going to be in the crash. We would have died together. I began to glorify God for sparing my life as I walked back to the house. I thought over and over about if

I had not left my phone in the house, I would have been in this car. If he had not left me, both of us were going to be in the crash. God took me from this car for a reason. Sometimes we may feel let down by somebody and it appears that our trip was canceled for nothing. It is a reason unknown to us, but God knows all. His plans will always be more beautiful and greater than all our disappointments.

BECOMING HOMELESS

After my roommate died, the property owner put me out of the house because it was a house assisted by a government program under my roommate's name. I was then assisted by another friend and he let me stay at his place until I could get my own place.

By this time, I had gotten another vehicle. One day, while in the process of looking for my own place, I was pulled over by the police and they issued me a ticket for driving with my high beam lights on. The court information was sent to my old address unknown to me. Since I did not see it, I did not appear in court. The court suspended my driver's license. Here I was now in the United States without a place to live and unable to drive.

A few days later, my friend told me I had to leave from his house because he needed his privacy. I was now on the streets with no car and no place to live. The only hope I had at that moment was I remained working for the nursing registry. During the time I would go to work, I would ask my manager if they needed me to stay overnight to work a double. If she said yes, I would spend the night there working. If she said no, I would stay and sleep in the break room. I was doing that until one night at 1:45am, the job police came and saw me sleeping in the break room. They asked me if I was working that night. I said yes, I am working. They went and asked the supervisor and she said to them I was not working that night. The job police came back and told me to leave that night. When I got outside, there was no more public transportation running at that time. I went to sleep under one of the upstairs buildings until the next morning.

I slept at many different friend's houses for a few nights here and there. This went on for almost 3 weeks until I was able to rent a room for myself.

CHAPTER 8

U.S. Education

WHEN I STARTED APPLYING for jobs, I applied for a career opportunity with many companies which would allow someone to continue their education in school before getting the job. When I sent in my applications for a job opportunity, I did not know these were going to school institutions. These institutions started emailing and calling me to take advantage of the programs they had. From those emails and phone call explanations, I was encouraged to visit one of the colleges. It was called Heald College.

When I visited this college campus, I went directly to the academic office. The academic office gave me great encouragement. They told me how the school was going to pay for my education to study in the IT Technician Program. I looked at this as a great opportunity to sign up and pursue my college education. They sent me to the financial aid department. I did not realize that when I signed for financial aid, I was signing my name to a large loan that I would have to start paying back six weeks after my graduation. The financial aid department did not explain the process to me clearly.

At that time, being new in the United States I did not completely know the difference between a loan and a grant. The Heald College financial aid department was not clear because their interest was to get as many students as possible with financial loans to increase funding for the school. When I started attending this college, I realized some unusual activities in the school within the first and second semester. I found that there were a lot of perks for students who had applied for $15,000 United States dollars and above in financial aid. These students would be given good grades even if they did not work hard for them. These students were also offered awards.

Awards included borrowing the school laptop to take home on the weekend, receiving a grocery card for food, or using a coupon for free food in the student cafeteria. All these motivations and free gifts were only given to students who signed up for student loans. I was given a best dressed student award twice and the most behaved student award three times. I was also given many grades that I know I did not deserve in the school. The academic department decided to give me my textbooks free without any money payments. I did not know that these textbooks were charged on my account along with the $20,000 dollar student loan.

One day, I decided to tell the school that I was taking a semester off to go on a vacation. The school administration wanted me to sign a form stating that if I did not return in the fall, I would be responsible for paying back the loan I had. I told them I had never signed for a loan that needed to be paid back. The financial aid department said to me, "Yes, you have a loan to be paid back." My wife, who was my fiancée at that time, asked them why he must sign a form like that before going on a vacation. The response from them was because they wanted to reserve my space and continue to provide me with the supplies needed as a student at the school.

My American fiancée who knew something strange was going on, was at the school with me. The school officials told her to excuse us. They wanted to discuss these issues with me privately. My fiancée walked out of the office shouting in her loud voice, "Daniel, don't sign any document!" I did not know that the school was about to close, and this is why they wanted me to sign such a form. Every form they offered me to sign, I refused to sign it. The chairman for the financial aid department said to me, "Whatever it is, whether you sign the form or not, you are still going to be responsible to pay back the money."

I begin to wonder why it was that I had not graduated, and the school was coming after me so strong with money issues. I left the school campus with my fiancée to go home. After my one-month vacation, I decided to go on the campus to resume school. When I got there, I did not see any students, only a load of trucks with all the school equipment. I asked someone who was around, "Is the school relocating?" They said, "The school has been permanently closed by the government."

MY FEDERAL STUDENT LOAN

After Heald College was permanently closed by the State of California, I decided to wait for the year to end before deciding what to do about my school. It was 2014. Months later I received a letter in my mailbox from Heald College showing me a start date for paying back a student loan in the amount of $20,800.00 will begin September 2014. I ignored the notice and continued to pray to the Almighty God for His intervention. I decided to continue my education in the nursing career at San Francisco City College. When the time came for me to start making payments for Heald, I did not send any payment. I received several letters from Heald College but did not respond to them. I continued to pray and ask God for His decision.

One day I called them and asked what student loan they are talking about. They said the loan I signed for at Heald college for the IT Technician Program. I said I did not graduate and furthermore, the school closed on me. I cannot pay that money. This unpaid debt from that loan was on my credit and made my score low. I received so many calls from the credit collection company, but I did not respond to them. I continued to pray.

I went to San Francisco City College to sign off for school, but they refused my Heald College grade credits and to accept me in the school. I asked them why my application had been denied by the school. They said there has been a hold on my education in California until the student loan I owed Heald College was completely paid for. I left and went home. I decided to make many calls to get help from the State of California and anyone else. The only thing they told me was half of my student loan could be removed if I am unemployed or if I had a disability, but I was employed and not disabled so I could not qualify for this.

I did not know what to do but continued to pray to God for help. On the second day of February 2015, I received a call from the State of California that my student loan had been canceled. Before the year ended, I received a letter from the Department of Education in California that stated all student loans I owed with Heald college were canceled and whatever money I paid to Heald College would be refunded back to me in a check. This is how God delivered me out of a $20,000 dollar student loan debt.

CHAPTER 9

A Blessed Life

As I reflect on my life, many things have transpired since my early years living in Liberia and in the United States. I am thankful to God for all He has done for me through this difficult journey. He helped me to graduate from high school. I have traveled to the United States to live and marry a beautiful, wonderful woman of God. I have been blessed with seven living children. He has provided me with a wonderful job at the VA hospital.

I have been protected from so many accidents. God has opened many doors for me, and I have been able to be a blessing to my family in Liberia during this time. I have been given so much favor. God has also blessed me with wonderful spiritual leaders who have helped me in my journey of faith, righteous living, and knowing God better. Moses Drooh, Roderick Gittens, and Benjamin Marshall have been incredible role models for me. Everything I have needed, God has provided. Here are a few more episodes from my life to make my point.

MEETING MY WIFE

> *"The Lord God said it is not good for the man to be alone I will make a helper suitable for him."*
>
> *Genesis 2:18*

Charlotte my wife was and is my rib bone. In California while working at the Veteran Affairs Hospital through an agency, I met my beautiful wife Charlotte. I did not know that she could ever become my wife. She was the person who would supervise workers in the mental health department on night shift. When I started this job, I did not know how to do the job correctly, but each time I would report to work, she would guide and help me to know what I was supposed to do. Working two jobs, I would at times be very sleepy and tired which was making it hard for me to stay awake, but Charlotte would try to help keep me awake to avoid me getting in trouble and being fired from my job.

There was one time me and a fellow Liberian co-worker was working the same shift, we decided to take our breaks in one of the empty patient's rooms. We had blankets and pillows laid on the floor to take a nap. We did not think anything was wrong with doing that. She came into the room doing her hourly rounds and saw us sleeping. She said to us, "Get up, you can't sleep in here, if they catch you, they will fire you immediately." This was the beginning of many helps Charlotte gave me.

My wife would help me to adjust to the culture of America. As my friend, she and her family helped me move when I got kicked out of a room I was renting after losing my job. When my father died, she and her family gave money to help with burial cost. As I began to see her as more than just my friend, God gave me a dream about her. In this dream, I was standing behind a big, round rock trying to get over it to the other side, but because this rock was so big and round, I could not easily hold on and get over it. While I was wondering how to get over it, I saw Charlotte standing on this round rock. She reached down to me, I grabbed her hand, and she pulled me over to a flat level rock and I was by her side. As we stood there together, I looked over and saw large numbers of black ants. They were coming after me. Charlotte said to me "Run Daniel!" As I ran off, I came and stopped at a place of beautiful flowers.

FAVOR WITH MY JOB

Working in the medical field, God has blessed me with so much favor among my patients, co-workers, managers, and supervisors. While working in the hospital through the registry agency, I was offered a full-time position by the manager without applying for the job.

Many patients had written so many compliments and letters of me being a good worker. I was blessed to receive the Best Employee Award on three occasions.

TIME TO MOVE

When I was in Liberia, the place I had always wanted to live in when I traveled to the United States was San Francisco. It was a childhood dream to live there one day and God answered my prayers. When I married my wife, I joined her to live in the City of San Francisco where she was already living with her two young adult children.

After three years, the living condition began to get uncomfortable for us. The house we lived in was old with mold and mildew growing on the walls and the windows. This made it a very unsafe place for us. We decided to move and even though we did not know where to move, we would not wait anymore. We told our two young adult children that we were ready to leave, but they did not want to leave just yet because everything was convenient. We were all close to our jobs, stores, and church. We were able to save more money with the four of us working and paying the bills together. They tried to convince us to stay longer, even one more year, but we could not bear it any longer.

During this time, God gave me a dream. God gives me dreams all the time. In this dream, there was a large dead dry tree standing by me and my wife with our two adult children. Suddenly this large tree started to fall in our direction. The dead tree was coming to us so quickly that we could barely escape from it hitting us. My wife and I went one way, and our two children went the other way. The tree fell between us, separating us. The bottom part of this tree went up in the air and fell between my son and daughter, separating them. I told my wife this dream and she told me she believed God was saying in this dream, "Now is the time to leave!"

My wife and I checked for a place in San Francisco for two weeks, but we could not find a place. We went to another city to search. The first day of our search, we were accepted by the landlord immediately without any background check. Within the next two weeks, we moved to this city temporarily for the next six months, until God could show us where to go permanently.

During this time, we began to fellowship with the pastor God connected us with when we last traveled back to visit Liberia. His church was in Sacramento, two hours away. We felt led by God to move there. We informed our pastor in San Francisco of our desire to move and prayed with the pastor in Sacramento in faith to move where he was. We began to work on transferring our jobs to the VA hospital in that city. I applied for an opening on the job board. My supervisor did not want me to go and tried to prevent it, but through God's favor all the doors opened for me to transfer. It was amazingly smooth and fast.

My wife had been working for twenty-two years at her place of employment in the city of San Francisco. She applied for an open job in Sacramento and ended up getting promoted to a new position. Both of us were now scheduled to work at our new location. Me and my wife had our prayers answered in a short time.

The only thing left to do was to find a place to live in Sacramento. We were blessed to move five minutes away from our new spiritual leader through his referral. God also blessed our two children with their own places. God is amazing. We put our trust in Him. We prayed for His perfect will. He provided for everything and we were very satisfied.

MY PRAYER LIFE

Today, I am spending more time with God in prayer. Me and my wife pray together. My prayer life has grown strong. I have prayed for many people including many of the patients that I have worked with. There have been great answers in those prayers.

When I was working at Sutter Hospital, a patient was admitted for a liver transplant. He spent months going from hospital to hospital. A new liver could not be found for him by doctors. One day, I felt the spirit of God strong on me to pray for this patient. After I got through praying for him. I spoke over his life that God was going to heal him in a week. In that same week, the patient called me and said that they had found a new liver for him. The patient, his family, and I began to glorify God in his room. After receiving his new liver and getting better, he went home with his family. I have spoken with this man several times. He always tells me that God has worked everything out for him perfectly.

TRAVELING BACK HOME

After eight years of being in America, God connected me to a Liberian pastor named Moses Drooh. He and his wife Debra had a love and vision to go back to Liberia and minister the word of God to the people. My wife and I traveled with them. This was the first time I was able to go back and see family. I was so excited to see my family and friends. They were happy to see me as well.

Since that time, God has blessed me to be able to travel back and forth to Liberia several times with Pastor Benjamin Marshall under his mission ministry. He brings the love and word of

God to so many orphaned children in Liberia. I am so blessed to be able to return to my native land and share my story with so many young people.

CLOSING SUMMARY

THE CHANGING OF CATERPILLARS into butterflies is known as METAMORPHOSIS. Metamorphosis is the process of transformation from an immature form to an adult form in several distinct stages. It could be a change in the form or nature of a thing; a person is changed into a completely different one by natural or supernatural means.

There are several stages in human life, but three are most important for our success. The three stages are known as morning, afternoon, and evening. Before your dream can come to pass, you will need to go through these stages and have a full understanding of all of them.

In human life, the morning stage is known as childhood. In this stage, one does not even know anything about his or herself and life.

Every success depends on someone's effort. The afternoon stage is known as boyhood or teenage world. In this stage, the human mind becomes well-developed in good or bad. The evening stage is known as man or adulthood. This stage is where we should put together all the good ideas we have developed during our growth and know who we are and where we are mentally and spiritually.

Growing up as a child, I knew one day I would have my own family and take care of the responsibilities God had for me as a man. I learned that a responsible man guides and provides for the people under his care emotionally, physically, and spiritually. I became greatly encouraged when I was promoted to the 10th grade and my Bible teacher read to the class the scripture, "I can do all things through Christ who strengthens me." (Philippians 4:13)

Some people think that growth in life is limited to you becoming older. When people grow in age, they may grow physically taller, bigger, and stronger; however, I believe withstanding hardship and temptations bring about the best growth in someone's life. At times, it comes with multiple failures, rejections, and disappointments but if we keep our focus on what we want and press forward with a positive attitude, we will always be an overcomer and not a failure.

We must understand that failure is not the alternative to success, it is only a temporary setback on the way to something much bigger. Failure is something we want to avoid, but everybody encounters failure at one point or another. What truly matters is how we react to it and learn from it. This is what will define our true success or failure. Our failure with one thing does not mean we are a total failure. Rather, sometimes it means there is a bigger opportunity ahead.

We will face some circumstances in our lives for God to take glory in. One thing we need to know is: He is an expert at bringing good out of every bad situation. He will use any circumstance to fulfill His purpose. God will always turn our disappointment into a day of improvement. Do not accept defeat based on how you feel. Do not let your present condition be your destination. Keep trying, keep pressing, and keep believing there is a better day ahead in Jesus.

CPSIA information can be obtained
at www.ICGtesting.com
Printed in the USA
FSHW022057230321
79697FS